WISDOM
FOR A CHANGING WORLD

WISDOM
FOR A CHANGING WORLD

Wisdom in Old Testament Theology

* * *

Ronald E. Clements

* * *

BERKELEY LECTURES 2

BIBAL Press
Berkeley, California 94701
1990

BERKELEY LECTURE SERIES

1. Norbert F. Lohfink, S.J.
   Options for the Poor: The Basic Principle of Liberation Theology in the Light of the Bible (BIBAL Press, 1987)

2. Ronald E. Clements
   Wisdom for a Changing World: Wisdom in Old Testament Theology (BIBAL Press, 1990)

Library of Congress Cataloging-in-Publication Data

Clements, R. E. (Ronald Ernest) 1929-
    Wisdom for a Changing World: wisdom in Old Testament theology
    Ronald E. Clements
        p.   cm. -- (Berkeley lectures; 2)
    The Bailey lectures delivered April 17-18, 1989, Berkeley, Calif.
    ISBN 0-941037-13-4 (pbk.) : $7.95
        1. Wisdom literature--Criticism, interpretation, etc. 2. Bible.
BS1455.C57   1990   89-62248
  223'.06--dc20   CIP

Copyright © 1990 BIBAL Press, Berkeley, CA 94701
Printed by GRT Book Printing, Oakland, CA 94601

CONTENTS

Editor's Foreword   7

Preface: John W. Bailey and the Bailey Lectures   9

I.   Wisdom in a Theological Context 15

    A.   The International Origins of Wisdom
    B.   Wisdom and the Israelite Community
    C.   Wisdom and Piety

II.   Death, Life and Healing 37

    A.   Wisdom as the Path of Life
    B.   The Significance of Sickness and Healing
         in Post-Exilic Wisdom

III. Wisdom and the Royal Court 57

    A.   The King as Exemplary Wise Man
    B.   Solomon as the Ideal Wise King
    C.   Wisdom and Kingship in a Gentile Setting

EDITOR'S FOREWORD

Studying in Berkeley is exhilarating, at least in part, because of the constant stream of outstanding lecturers and visiting scholars from all over the world. As one of my students put it recently, "If I attended all the lectures that interested me here in the GTU (Graduate Theological Union) and at UCB (University of California at Berkeley), I would never complete my regular studies." Though this statement was an exaggeration, the point was clear; for the lecture fare in Berkeley is rich indeed. This particular series of publications is an attempt to distribute the content of some of the more worthy lectures presented in Berkeley to the wider audience they deserve.

Ronald Clements is the best known Baptist scholar of the Old Testament in Europe at the present time. He is currently the Davidson Professor of Old Testament at King's College, University of London. He earned his degrees at Spurgeon's College in London; Christ's College, Cambridge; and the University of Sheffield, where he received his Ph.D. in 1961. After lecturing seven years at the University of Edinburgh, he spent 1967-83 as a lecturer at Cambridge University. An ordained Baptist minister in England since 1956, he has written a dozen significant books on the Old Testament.

On April 17-18, 1989, Ronald Clements delivered the Bailey Lectures in Berkeley, which were jointly sponsored by the American Baptist Seminary of the West and the Church Divinity School of the Pacific. Those lectures are here edited into a more popular format for publication.

We are happy to include this volume as the second in our BERKELEY LECTURE SERIES. The first volume in this series appeared in 1987 under the title *Option for the Poor: The Basic Principle of Liberation Theology in Light of the Bible,* by Norbert F. Lohfink, S.J. That book has now been reviewed in some 14 academic journals across the world, in five different languages. C. S. Rodd, in his review in *The Expository Times,* described it as "a book which I hope all ministers and theological students will regard as compulsory reading, and I would like to think that many lay people will read it as well. Here are the considered views of one of the leading Continental Old Testament scholars, written simply." The same could be said of Ronald Clements' book, which we hope will also enjoy the wide circulation it deserves.

The Berkeley Institute of Bible, Archaeology & Law (BIBAL) was established to fund and administer projects in the area of biblical studies, including both archaeology and special work on the connections between modern Anglo/American and civilian jurisprudence and the legal materials in the Bible. The institute is a religious nonprofit corporation in the State of California whose projects include research, excavation, teaching and publication. In matters of publication our interests focus on works in biblical literature, biblical archaeology, and Bible and law. Ronald Clements' *Wisdom for a Changing World* is a stimulating study of the wisdom literature of ancient Israel. The book is proof of a reputation well merited and evidence of how deeply the author has reflected on Wisdom. We are proud to include this volume among our growing list of titles. For a complete list of current titles, see the last page of this book.

Duane L. Christensen, President
Berkeley Institute of Bible, Archaeology & Law

PREFACE

JOHN W. BAILEY (1873-1969)

The Bailey Lectures at the American Baptist Seminary of the West are given annually to honor a distinguished New Testament scholar, Professor John W. Bailey, who taught at the seminary for 32 years and was Professor of New Testament Interpretation, and in retirement became professor emeritus.

Dr. John W. Bailey was born in 1873 in Indiana and died in Berkeley at the age of 96—on June 6, 1969. He graduated from Franklin College in 1898. He earned his B.D. in 1901 and his Ph.D. *magna cum laude* in 1904 from the University of Chicago. He served pastorates in Illinois, Wisconsin, and Iowa, and then became president of Central College in Pella, Iowa. Later he was president of Colorado Woman's College in Denver.

While Dr. Bailey taught in Berkeley, the seminary was known as the Berkeley Baptist Divinity School. He authored six books in the field of biblical studies and was a contributor to *The Interpreter's Bible* (on Thessalonians). In retirement he continued to teach for nine years at the seminary, and served as an interim pastor, author, and book reviewer.

For more than 30 years Dr. Bailey taught an adult Bible class at the First Baptist Church of Berkeley. That class established a fund which became the financial resource for the Bailey Lectures. When Louise Bailey died, additional gifts in her memory strengthened the Bailey Lecture Fund.

John W. Bailey
(1873-1969)

President Sanford Fleming at the Berkeley Baptist Divinity School spoke appreciatively of Dr. Bailey's "profound scholarship," and said that he gave "his students an understanding and appreciation which brought personal enrichment and prepared them to preach and teach (the Bible) intelligently and persuasively."

Through the years outstanding scholars have been invited to present the Baily Lectures in Berkeley. Among them have been Georg Braulik, Walter Brueggemann, Robert Guelich, William Herzog, Norbert Lohfink, Dale Moody, Ross Snyder, and Barrie White.

Dr. Ronald Clements' stimulating and thought-provoking lectures in April 1989 continued a rich tradition of serious scholarship and application to life situations. We are delighted to add his contribution to the BERKELEY LECTURE SERIES.

WISDOM
IN OLD TESTAMENT THEOLOGY

CHAPTER ONE

WISDOM IN A THEOLOGICAL CONTEXT

"Whence then comes wisdom? And where is the place of understanding?" So runs the questioning of Job 28:20 in what is almost certainly a relatively late reflection on the mystery and majesty of wisdom. The two questions, however, also serve to focus attention upon two central issues for the study of the wisdom tradition of the Hebrew Bible. Where did Israelite wisdom originate? Were its roots to be traced to the popular realms of folk-learning and the education of young men in the circle of the extended family? Or was it a more sophisticated expertise nurtured in the scribal and administrative activities of the royal court? Or should we think with some scholars of an ancient and deeply rooted tradition of education which gave rise to schools and classes of young people being prepared for the rigors of life? Each of these views seems to contain some element of truth, and yet each of them fails to provide a truly comprehensive explanation for the many-sidedness of Israelite wisdom.

We can also ask, "Where is the place of understanding?", not simply rhetorically as part of a concern to emphasize the divine source and origin of wisdom, but in the more human and modern context of asking where we are to place wisdom in the overall context of a biblical theology. Have those biblical theologians been right who have focused so much attention upon the fact that the wisdom tradition of ancient Israel appears to stand outside the primary concerns of covenant, nation, and election? These topics otherwise represent the center, and cohesive cement, of an Old Testament theology.

The International Origins of Wisdom

We may begin by drawing attention to certain important features about wisdom which can then serve to clarify the way in which the following argument is developed. The first of these is that wisdom certainly did not first originate in Israel, but is richly and instructively present in the surviving traditions of the ancient Near East generally. Especially in Egypt the pursuit of *ma'at* (= "order") represented a major part of the quest for understanding the world, coping with its many mysteries and hazards, and for achieving success in its varied opportunities. In Mesopotamia also, the search for wisdom gave rise to some moving and memorable reflections upon the dangers and meaning of life, and to the building up of expertise in facing life's problems and fashioning success and happiness out of the ever-present risk of failure and darkness. Where the cultus was almost wholly absorbed in the magical, and semi-magical, preoccupation with discerning omens, interpreting dreams, and avoiding the danger of offending deities whose will was often inscrutable, wisdom sought for a more reasoned truth. So in a real sense wisdom was old by the time that it entered Israel, even if we give full credence to the biblical claim that such wisdom found its first, and most illustrious, patron and skilled practitioner in the person of Solomon.

We shall have opportunity to note that there are reasons for doubting the historical veracity of Solomon's personal reputation as a composer of proverbs and a searcher after wisdom. Nevertheless, there is no reason whatsoever for not believing as true the claim that, from the days when the monarchy began in Israel with David and Solomon, Israel was familiar with a tradition of wisdom teaching and began to develop its own ways of nurturing its pursuit and encouraging its preservation. Wisdom came to be as much a part of Israel's life as psalmody became part of the expression of worship and collections of written law formed a part of the judicial procedures that administered justice. In a very real sense, the claim that Solomon was a unique patron and practitioner of wisdom is somewhat irregular and paradoxical. In the deepest sense wisdom needed no famed teacher to lend it authority, since its very nature declared that its authority lay within itself. It affirmed its teachings, not because an inspired teacher of the past had brought them to light, but because they were true, as tested in the fires of experience. They were minted in the hardest of all furnaces—that of life itself! It is clear, however, from Egyptian texts that wisdom did sometimes draw to itself great and famous names, although seldom those of the most famous kings, such as Solomon. Amen-em-ope, Onchsheshonqy and others are names of important officials that became attached to Egyptian wisdom writings. Even here, however, it is never wholly clear how far these major named figures were collectors of wisdom which they culled from many sources, or whether they were primarily themselves composers of such teachings. We may reflect in connection with Hammurabi's famed law code that his name became attached to it as the senior administrator of the realm, rather than because he was himself an individual exponent of jurisprudence. However, most of the Babylonian wisdom writings that have come down to us are anonymous.

This strong international flavor of Israelite wisdom has appeared to pose a problem for biblical scholars, especially since the recognition that we have in chapters 22-24 of the book of Proverbs a direct adaptation to Israelite needs of a substantial section of the Egyptian Wisdom of Amen-em-ope. This single demonstrable case, however, simply illustrates the wider fact that, so far as the collectors and teachers of wisdom were concerned, truth, wherever it was to be found, was worth having and could be incorporated into the usable literature of the wise. Israel had no monopoly upon it, and only at a relatively late stage in its development was there a deep concern to bring this tradition of wisdom into harmony with the tradition of a Mosaic *torah*. The time came when wisdom needed formally to be baptized in name, if not always in spirit, to the tradition of Israel's faith as a unique disclosure to one nation alone of the truth about God, man, and the world. For a tradition of biblical theology which placed great emphasis upon categories of uniqueness and distinctiveness as primary facets of the revelatory content of the biblical material, such close links with an older Near Eastern environment appeared prejudicial to the authority of wisdom.

What I am concerned to argue is that it was precisely this uniquely international origin of wisdom, its claim to express universally valid truths, and not least to present a teaching about life that knew no national boundaries, nor based itself upon a single revelatory act of the past, that made wisdom so important to Israel in the post-exilic period. When we look at the Old Testament wisdom tradition there seems to be little effective basis for doubting the fact that all three of the major wisdom writings of the Hebrew Bible—Proverbs, Job and Ecclesiastes—were products, in their final form, of the post-exilic age. Of these, only the book of Proverbs contains a substantial collection of older proverbial teaching. Some of this is formulated in the full proverb form and much of it in the sentence type of admonition, and both of these certainly had their origins in the pre-exilic era. More room for questioning the time of origin exists over the longer discourse admonitions that appear in Prov 1-9, which must surely have been written, as a literary unit, from the beginning. In spite of recent attempts to find an early date for these on account of their content, their composition in the post-exilic age is adopted here as by far the most likely time of their origin. This is not to deny that wisdom found early entry into Israel, possibly already acquiring significant prestige as early as Solomon's time, but to recognize that it took on a different purpose and function in the post-exilic period from that which it enjoyed in its earlier pre-exilic setting. From being a rather elitist and highly distinctive pursuit of a minority, with a central focus in the royal court, it became a vital teaching medium for every Jew.

Nor do I think that we can regard it as a mere historical accident that the three Old Testament writings which show the clearest evidence of the influence of the Hellenization of Jewish thought—Ecclesiastes, Ben Sira (Ecclesiasticus) and Wisdom of Solomon—were wisdom writings. Of course this can be explained in part as a consequence of a certain similarity of style and subject matter between Greek philosophy and Israelite wisdom. Wisdom itself could appear as a kind of "philosophy," and the extent to which Greek thought had isolated and evaluated ethics as a distinctive branch of human understanding relating to conduct, meant that wisdom inevitably shared a large area of overlap with these philosophical interests.

Yet more than this was at issue, since it was a vital feature of the development of a concern with wisdom in creation as it is presented in Prov 8:22-31, that this wisdom was universal in its range and authority. Hitherto the almost exclusive concern of scholars with this cosmic role of wisdom has been with its personification as a female figure, possibly originally as a goddess, and with the femininity of wisdom. Yet this was certainly not the central intellectual feature that has motivated the development of this imagery, and may have been little more than a convenient literary device. In fact, the primary feature of this poem celebrating the role of wisdom in creation is the strong emphasis that it places upon the cosmic range and authority of wisdom. There is no place on earth or in heaven where the writ of wisdom does not run. All things in heaven and earth conform to the canons of wisdom, because without her there was not anything made that was made. This is, of course, to draw into the imagery of wisdom a feature that was applied later to the idea of *logos*. There is, however, no doubt at all that it is the same fundamental assertion of universal cosmic authority that was being made. What form the symbolism of wisdom should take, whether as feminine or as an impersonal force, as *logos* essentially was, remains secondary to this primary concern.

A starting-point for the understanding of the distinctive theological contribution of wisdom is to be found in this grounding of it in a concept of *cosmos* that made it an indispensable intellectual tool for post-exilic Israel. It was precisely because it was not a branch of truth grounded in a tradition of election and covenant, and focused exclusively upon the concept of Israel as a nation, that made its contribution so invaluable. Wisdom did not present its claim to recognition and observance on the basis of Israel's existence as a nation—a *goy* among other *goyim* . Instead it made its appeal for acceptance to all who would hear its claims to be grounded in the nature of the world itself. Hence it could address its promised benefits to Jews who found themselves part of a wider, and often scattered, community who inhabited a God-created universal order.

This was important precisely because Judaism had become a faith and a religious tradition that was no longer the perquisite of one nation, but was being expressed through Jews who belonged to many nations. So much of the inhibiting legacy of a tradition of critical biblical scholarship which has focused primarily upon the history of Israel as a nation, and upon its religion as a national religion, has been its consequent devaluing of the experience and developments of the Jewish diaspora.

It is striking that we have come to speak freely of the "post-exilic" period of Israel's religious development. Yet in historical reality this is itself a rather over-strained use of language. The "exile" did not properly come to an end, in that there ceased to be any significant part of the Jewish religious community living outside the boundaries of the land, even if we consider this latter in its wider signification. Exile passed, by a series of largely unrecorded stages, into a larger and more permanent existence of Jewish dispersion. The same word—*golah*—is used to describe this. We focus attention upon the developments that took place in Judah and Jerusalem, but at the same time we know that the most important of these developments found their inspiration and leadership from Jews of the *golah* .

It is as we trace this historical spread of Judaism into dispersion out of the survivors of the Babylonian exile, that we can see how wisdom provided a primary tool for Judaism's survival. When we ask about the setting-in-life of the Pentateuch as a whole, and of the shaping of the prophetic canon as a collected unity, we must recognize that the setting for both was provided by the recognition that Judaism was no longer a single nation but embraced a large and thriving diaspora.

It is in this context that we can see that the primary religious and political question that faced post-exilic Judaism was how it was to provide a bond that held together Jews in the "exile" of diaspora with the community that maintained control in Judah and Jerusalem. Dan 9:7 very skillfully describes the complexity of the range of the community that had arisen by the second century BCE:

> To thee, O Lord, belongs righteousness, but to us confusion of face, as at this day, to the men of Judah, to the inhabitants of Jerusalem, and to all Israel, those that are near and those that are far away, in all the lands to which thou hast driven them, because of the treachery which they have committed against thee.
>
> Dan 9:7

The very canonical shape of the Hebrew Bible, with *torah* at its head, has undoubtedly been fashioned to provide a body of instruction that did not disinherit either group. Narratives that recounted the divine gift of the land, the national constitution of Israel in the gift of kingship by which that nation was represented as a single entity, had all to be relegated to the realm of a prophetic eschatology. They are accordingly dealt with after the five books of *torah* in the Former and Latter

Prophets. For Judaism of the post-exilic age to have balanced the scales in favor of either the Jerusalem community with the temple at its center, or the exiles with their energy and progressiveness, would have resulted in a serious impairment of the felt spiritual realities of the situation. To have focused everything upon land, nationhood, and kingship, would have been to return to the situation as it was before the catastrophic events of the first two decades of the sixth century BCE. Yet to do this would have been to disinherit the larger segment of the Jewish community who were scattered among many nations. On the other hand, to have trusted everything to the power of God to "maintain the cause" (cf. 1 Kgs 8:49) indefinitely of those who had been driven into the exile of dispersion would have been to submit to an inevitable process of assimilation and spiritual atrophy. The final form of the Book of Isaiah represents a very carefully constructed work that seeks to hold together these two poles of spiritual aspiration. It presents Jerusalem at the center (cf. Isa 2:2-4; 10:24-27; 14:32; 63:1-5, etc.) but focuses major attention upon a congeries of dispersed Jewish communities awaiting God's signal to return (cf. Isa 11:11-16; 27:12-13; 60:1-14 etc.).

Where, we may ask, does wisdom fit in all this in such a way as to make it a tradition of primary significance? The answer to this question is to be found in the fact that wisdom formed a bridge between the older national institutions of Israel's life, where kingship and temple formed the primary focal points, and the new world of the diaspora.

Wisdom and the Israelite Community

It has been an important insight of biblical scholarship to recognize that the idea of the people of God in the book of Deuteronomy is oriented around the idea of Israel as a nation. This has been reinforced by more recent work upon the subject and would certainly find support in the idea that much of the Deuteronomic language and style is a result of its origin in circles closely linked to the administration of the state. This feature, however, serves to reinforce our awareness that up until the momentous year 587 BCE, the intellectual life of Israel, as it had emerged, rested within two main streams: the cultic, with its focus upon the temple and its verbal expression in psalmody, and the kingly, with its focus upon traditions of history and law. When the temple was destroyed and the Davidic kingship removed from the throne, not only were two visible symbols of the divine blessing of Israel taken from the scene, but the intellectual foundations of its corporate life undermined. The holiness that Israel enjoyed, the blessing that it sought and the curse that it prayed to avoid (cf. Deut 7:6-16), were intrinsic intellectual and cultural constructs of the temple cultus. Israel was a holy nation and this concept of holiness, regarded in a quasi-physical fashion as extending throughout the breadth of the nation and its land, formed the intellectual foundation for community life. Offenses against the community were considered to "defile" the land (cf. Ezek 36:16-21). In contrast, the maintenance of this holiness was the pathway to health and prosperity (Deut 7:14-15).

It is when we pause to think in terms of a situation in which Israel was no longer a nation that we realize how important it was that concepts of morality and social order should have foundations that stretched beyond the boundaries of nationhood. This is why wisdom became such an important aspect of Israel's intellectual and cultural heritage in the post-exilic age. We can then turn on its head the argument that wisdom's international origins, and its lack of primary reference to concepts of community and nationhood, that otherwise form so central a part of the religious ideas of the Old Testament, relegate it to the fringe of Old Testament theology. On the contrary it is precisely the absence of this national frame of reference that lends to biblical wisdom its great importance.

We need to frame the form of the argument carefully here, since it is not our contention that wisdom was either dogmatically universalistic in its original setting, or that it consciously rejected the national dimension of Israel's life. Wisdom found a home for itself in pre-exilic Israel, and acquired associations and ideals appropriate to the national life of Israel. Primarily we would contend that this home was provided by the life and administrative circles of the Jerusalem court which was necessarily nationalistic in its moral and social assumptions. Nevertheless, what was of importance was that wisdom had established a tradition of social instruction and morality which sought to ground its teachings in the created order of the world. Originally therefore it simply took for granted the national dimension of Israel's life and the national functioning of Israel's religion. It did not deny this national dimension, but yet it seldom drew reference to it into the fundamental fabric of its admonitions and insights (although we may cf. Prov 14:28, 34).

We can discover the significance of this distinctive stance taken by wisdom toward the order of life by contrasting it with the way in which certain fundamental human standards are defended in the older literature by appeal to the phrase "such and such an action is not done in Israel." This is the case in Tamar's appeal to Amnon in 2 Sam 13:12 that he should not rape her, and this assumption also underlies the account of the rape of the Levite's concubine in Judg 19:20; 20:10, etc. In early Israel, the moral code was supported by the ethics of kinship in which notions of the honor and integrity of the larger tribal community governed the behavior of each of its members. There was no separate conception of purely individual human dignity as such, nor of human rights in a universal sense, since all codes of conduct were channelled through the family and clan and the larger tribal community to which these belonged. Clearly in the era in which Deuteronomy emerged most large communities could be divided into three classes: the fellow-Israelite, the sojourner (*ger*), and the complete outsider (*nokhri'*). A striking expression of the consequence of this classification is to be seen in the regulation controlling the disposal of the carcass of a dead animal that may be found (Deut 15:21).

Such a manner of controlling social and moral actions is all very well where the categories of *ger* and *nokhri'* are exceptions, and encountered only seldom. It became an entirely different situation when the roles were reversed and large numbers of Jews found themselves forced to live as aliens and foreigners in other lands. The needs of morality were no less pressing, but the appeals to national and clan identity could no longer sustain their original authority. Precisely because wisdom had entered into Israel as an international pursuit, it provided a new principle of authority for the recognition and sanctioning of morality. Beyond the ethic of the clan and of the nation, wisdom established an ethic grounded in creation itself and valid for all humanity. It addressed its teachings to persons as members of the human race, and not as members of a specific clan, or even a national community. Consequently it could recognize no valid distinction between fellow-Israelites, resident aliens (strangers), and foreigners. To communities that now found themselves more or less permanent aliens in foreign lands, this grounding of morality in creation itself, which wisdom advocated, was of prime significance.

In this connection we can note how relevant and valuable are the insights of the social anthropologist Victor Turner regarding the "betwixt and between" status of those who find themselves living under provisional circumstances and which he has described as a condition of "liminality." Building upon the observations of various *rites de passage* in which young men of a tribe are set apart for a period of initiation and discipline before entering adulthood, Turner discerned in such experiences analogies to Christian pilgrimages. Such a period of withdrawal from the normal obligations of life, separation from all but a few of one's fellow citizens, and return to the community in a modified and enhanced status, all conform to A. van Gennep's observations regarding such transition rites.

This state of "liminality" draws attention to the suspension of normal codes of conduct, the sense of living under a peculiarly *special* set of rules, the close bonding that takes place between those who are participants in the transitional experience, and a consequent heightened sense of *belonging* to the larger community.

Our argument is that this was essentially the situation that faced those who found themselves driven out from their homeland into a condition of "exile," which was gradually transformed into a more or less permanent condition of dispersion. The older categories of clan, tribal and national obligations fell into a state of suspension, before the more immediate sense of obligation generated by the condition of "liminality" into which these exiles had passed. Wisdom then provided a fundamental basis of appeal and of moral obligation which took on new meaning in the community. Faced with the tensions between living in a totally enclosed isolation, or succumbing to absorption into the larger Gentile world which encompassed it, each Jewish community in diaspora had to come to terms with a relatively stable and on-going condition of "liminality."

In such a setting wisdom, from being a relatively modest and leisured pursuit of a privileged minority within the Israel of the monarchic period, became the groundwork for rethinking and re-establishing fundamental patterns of conduct, piety, and personal ambition in a non-national setting. From being a pursuit almost exclusively tied to the royal court and its dependants, wisdom became the pursuit of every Jew. What we discover therefore is that it provided radical changes in ideas of law, family ethic, and piety which subsequently left its mark upon Jewish faith in a very far-reaching way. Although, therefore, wisdom did not originate in post-exilic Jewish life, it was the needs of the post-exilic community which gave to wisdom its richest opportunity. At the same time, it is arguable that it was the inherited tradition of wisdom which offered to the post-exilic community of Judaism the intellectual tools for its survival.

It is important in this regard that we should recognize that the needs of the divided Jewish communities of the post-exilic era did not differ from each other in any dramatically different way. No doubt the restored community that held power and authority in Judah and Jerusalem during the fifth and fourth centuries BCE had, in the Jerusalem temple, the renewed symbol of religious authority and divine blessing. Yet the divided nature of this community is amply attested by the contents of the post-exilic prophetic writings. Knowledge of the needs of the diaspora have to be inferred, on account of the absence of documentary evidence, yet the shaping of the written *torah* provides us with some indispensable clues. It is also recognizable that the relatively late books of Esther and Daniel offer some significant insights into the problems that faced Jews living in diaspora.

Wisdom and Piety

In the most striking fashion we can see the outworking of this re-evaluation of notions of piety and morality in the wisdom instruction of Prov 10-25. To what extent this teaching has been retained in its oldest form, or has itself been subjected to modification and adaptation, can only be a matter of conjecture. Nevertheless, it seems probable that we are substantially presented here with early Israelite wisdom teaching, as much of the content implies, now preserved in a post-exilic framework. What is so striking, especially in the late material contained in this framework, is the manner in which fundamental concepts which had their origins in the cultus are extended in wholly new ways. At the same time, the preservation of these concepts in the teaching of the earlier wisdom serves to indicate that they were not a wholly new minting from the post-587 situation. It seems to be a case of old wine being poured into new bottles. We may confine ourselves here to a consideration of two of these concepts which appear as the most prominent: *viz.* those of "the fear of the Lord" and of "abomination."

That Israel was a "holy" nation appears as the most comprehensive of the earlier descriptions of Israel's unique national status as the people of the Lord (Yahweh). So it is given the foremost place in the constitutional affirmation:

> And you shall be to me a kingdom of priests and a holy nation.
>
> Exod 19:6

and:

> For you are a people holy to the Lord your God.
>
> Deut 7:6

To some degree the deuteronomic legislation, although it retains the concept of "holiness" as basic to Israel's status, modifies and interprets this in ways which indicate some element of distance from the more immediate cultic circle. Roughly contemporaneous with Deuteronomy we find that this older cultic language still appears with particular vigor and intensity in the Holiness Code (Lev 17-26). The idea of the holiness of the land informs very powerfully the extensive cultic and social polity of Lev 25 and this same notion of holiness is then put forward as the structural basis for Israel's entire range of conduct :

> So you shall keep my commandments and do them: I am the Lord.

And

> you shall not profane my holy name, but I will be treated as holy among the people of Israel; I am the Lord who makes you holy, who brought you out of the land of Egypt to be your God: I am the Lord.
>
> Lev 22:31-33

Over against this we find that in the teaching of Proverbs the language of holiness hardly appears at all. God is described as "the Holy One" in Prov 9:10 and 30:3; and in Prov 20:25 an affirmation that something is "holy" refers to the making of vows. Instead of holiness the concept of "the fear of the Lord" becomes for the teachers of wisdom the primary concept which is held to be the motivating impulse for all right acting and right thinking. Undoubtedly this phrase, like the language of holiness, was originally cultic in its origin. It signified simply one who was a *devotee* of the Lord, in the same way that others could be described as devotees, or *fearers* of other gods. Yet in the book of Proverbs, not only is the idea of fearing the Lord extended to cover a most extensive range of activities and attitudes, but such a concept has become the primary affirmation of the source and motive for acquiring wisdom. In the well known assertion of Prov 9:10:

> The fear of the Lord is the beginning of wisdom
> and the knowledge of the Holy One is insight.
> Prov 9:10

We may compare the closely related affirmation of Prov 1:7:

> The fear of the Lord is the beginning of knowledge;
> fools despise wisdom and instruction.

The reason why such fools behave badly and refuse the sages' instruction is then further elaborated:

> Because they hated knowledge
> and did not choose the fear of the Lord,
> would have none of my counsel,
> and despised all my reproof,
> therefore they shall eat the fruit of their way
> and be sated with their own devices.
> Prov 1:29-31

The extensive range of affirmations that follow from this primary conjunction of piety, in the form of the the fear of Yahweh, and wisdom as a socially desirable and life-preserving basis of conduct are then immense:

> The fear of the Lord is a fountain of life
>   that one may avoid the snares of death.
>   Prov 14:27

> Better is a little with the fear of the Lord
>   than great treasure and trouble with it.
>   Prov 15:16

> The fear of the Lord is instruction in wisdom,
>   and humility goes before honor.
>   Prov 15:33

> By loyalty and faithfulness iniquity is atoned for,
>   and by the fear of the Lord a man avoids evil.
>   Prov 16:6

> The fear of the Lord leads to life;
>   and he who has it rests satisfied;
>   he will not be visited by harm.
>   Prov 19:23

> The reward for humility and fear of the Lord
>   is riches and honor and life.
>   Prov 22:4

We should add to these broad affirmations those of Prov 2:5-8; 3:7, 11, 12, 26; 23:27; 24:21; 28:5, 14; and 31:30. For the authors of these sayings the idea of piety expressed in the phrase "the fear of the Lord" has become the primary sanction for all good conduct and for a love of the precepts of wisdom.

The benefits of long life and prosperity which ensue for those who maintain this attitude in life parallel very closely the benefits of health and welfare which the cultus had previously affirmed to be the rewards for those who observed the rules of holiness. This is especially noticeable, for example, when we compare the contrast between the benefits of living under obedience and blessing in Deut 28:1-14 or disobedience and curse in Deut 28:15-68.

It is clear that the authors of such proverbial sayings have found in the idea of reverence for God expressed through the notion of the "fear of Yahweh" a concept that was broader, and more suitable for their purposes, than that of "holiness." This was too cult-oriented, and too tied to a quasi-physical interpretation of conduct and proximity to the divine sphere, to cover the range that was needed. Such an idea of holiness inevitably carried with it the consciousness that to live in a place of exile was "to live in an unclean land" (cf. Amos 7:17). As a result, for the wisdom teachers the idea of holiness has been almost wholly replaced by the broader concept of "the fear of the Lord." This has proved to be more extensive in its range, more psychologically apposite and heart-searching in its demands, and more readily capable of application to every sphere of conduct. It represents a total way of life.

From being a relatively formalistic and cult-oriented concept, "the fear of the Lord" has become a fundamental descriptive formula for a way of life that is both pious in the religious sanctions which it recognizes, and yet highly moral in the conduct of which it approves. Our contention is that this was a distinctive feature of the way in which wisdom developed the ancient Israelite tradition, not because wisdom was inherently skeptical of cultus, for which there is little evidence, but because Israel's sages strove to find a more universalistic grounding for morality than the ancient concept of holiness offered. The initial origins of such a development may well have been pre-exilic, as seems in any case most probable, but it was the urgency of the situation created by the destruction of the temple as the cultic center of Israelite life in 587 BCE which raised such a shift of intellectual focus to a matter of major significance.

If the re-minting of the notion of holiness into a broader understanding of piety as a total way of life represents one way in which wisdom provided a bridge for a Jewish life beyond the borders of "the holy land," then the re-valuation of the idea of "abomination" represents another. It is, in effect, the reverse side of the notion of holiness. That which was an "abomination" (Heb.*to'ebah*) in ancient Israel was that which was unacceptable within the holy sphere of cultus. This is well illustrated in regard to the regulations governing the offering of the peace-offering (*shelem*) in Lev 19. The sacrificial meat of the offering is classed as unfit for eating by the third day after its slaughter:

> If it is eaten at all on the third day, it is an abomination; it will not be accepted, and every one who eats it shall bear his iniquity, because he has profaned a holy thing of the Lord; and that person shall be cut off from his people.
>
> Lev 19:7-8

In a similar vein we find that those animals which are classed as unfit for eating are described as constituting an "abomination" (cf. Lev 11:10, 11, 13, 20, etc.). That which is an abomination is that which contradicts the state of holiness and so cannot be accepted within the cultic sphere, or in the life of a nation which is itself "holy." An abomination renders a holy thing profane, although it is evident that each of the major terms used here does not have an exact modern counterpart in a world where even the concept of holiness has migrated far from its original meaning.

If we take as our starting-point the probability that it is the instructions of Prov 10-25 which form the oldest stratum of wisdom, then we may appropriately begin here:

A false balance is an abomination to the Lord,
　　but a just weight is his delight.
　　　　　　　　　　　　　　Prov 11:1

Men of perverse mind are an abomination to the Lord,
　　but those of blameless ways are his delight.
　　　　　　　　　　　　　　Prov 11:20

Lying lips are an abomination to the Lord,
　　but those who act faithfully are his delight.
　　　　　　　　　　　　　　Prov 12:22

The way of the wicked is an abomination to the Lord,
　　but he loves him who pursues righteousness.
　　　　　　　　　　　　　　Prov 15:9

The thoughts of the wicked are
　　an abomination to the Lord,
　　but the words of the pure are pleasing to him.
　　　　　　　　　　　　　　Prov 15:26

It is an abomination to kings to do evil,
　　for the throne is established by righteousness.
　　　　　　　　　　　　　　Prov 16:12

It is singularly noteworthy to find that it is the "thoughts" of the wicked, or their "perverse mind," or even their "way," as an abstract description of their mode of life, which are unacceptable to God. Similarly "lying lips" and a false balance are repudiated by him, all of which show that the concept of "abomination" has migrated far from its original cultic, and taboo-laden, setting. It is synonymous with "socially and morally reprehensible conduct." This broad generalizing extension of meaning for the term is then further demonstrated in the introduction to the book:

for the perverse man is an abomination to the Lord,
  but the upright are in his confidence.
                                                    Prov 3:32

Something of the concern to retain the notion of the cultic reference of "abomination" may be found in the saying:

The sacrifice of the wicked is an abomination;
  how much more when he brings it with evil intent.
                                                    Prov 21:27

Particularly noteworthy is the association of "abomination" with the sacrificial gift, but the classification as its rejection by God is wholly determined by the evil intent of the person who offers it. Pious intention has become the fundamental category by which the worth of a sacrificial offering is measured. A comparable intense moralizing of cultic practice is to be found in the saying concerning prayer, the simplest and most basic of all cultic activities:

The Lord is far from the wicked,
  but he hears the prayer of the righteous.
                                                    Prov 15:29

This recognition that the teachers of wisdom adopted a distant, and moderately critical attitude, towards the cultus has been widely recognized among scholars for some time. It has largely been regarded as a feature that was endemic to the whole Near Eastern tradition of wisdom. Yet there is little evidence of this. In any case it has also long been recognized that this intense moralizing and spiritualizing of cultic ideas and praxis is a peculiarly biblical phenomenon. It is distinctively Jewish, and has passed from its Jewish roots into the Christian Church. It has done much to sustain Jewish worship and piety over the centuries and has provided the intellectual substructure for the growth of a synagogal type of worship, which supplemented, and then replaced, the cultus of the Jerusalem temple. Our thesis therefore is that, although there were certain features in the wisdom tradition which made such a fundamental reinterpretation of cultus possible, it was the application of wisdom to the needs of Judaism after 587 BCE which led to the transformation. Wisdom reminted and reinvigorated the ideas and language of the cultus to suit the needs of scattered communities of Jews living in exile in order to show that "the fear of Yahweh" still stood as the foundation of all life.

CHAPTER TWO

DEATH, LIFE AND HEALING

There is a passage in the book of Ecclesiasticus from the Old Testament Apocrypha (Eccles 38:1-15) which is the first biblical description of the work of the physician in healing the sick in a way which relates directly to that of the modern medical profession. It will be helpful to begin by quoting a part of it:

Honor the physician with the honor due him, according to your need of him, for the Lord created him; for healing comes from the Most High, and he will receive a gift from the king. The skill of the physician lifts up his head, and in the presence of great men he is admired. The Lord created medicines from the earth, and a sensible man will not despise them.

Was not water made sweet with a tree in order that his power might be known? And he gave skill to men that he might be glorified in his marvellous works. By them he heals and takes away pain; the pharmacist makes of them a compound. His works will never be finished; and from him health is upon the face of the earth.

Eccles 38:1-8

This passage dates from ca. 190 BCE and, although it is
the first full biblical description of the work of the physician, it
comes at the end of a significant line of references in the book of
Proverbs to healing, medicine and health. Two features stand
out: the first of these is that the roles of both the physician and
the pharmacist are presented in a way that separates them from
the cultus. We cannot describe this as a truly secular interpretation of medicine and the healing art since the work of both
physician and pharmacist is each viewed as a gift of God, but it
is not a cultic ministry in any direct sense. A second feature is
that a concern with health and healing is accepted as a proper and
established part of the pursuit of wisdom. The healing art has
become an aspect of wisdom and a health-giving way of life is
dependent upon adhering to wisdom's precepts.

Healing and the Cultus

In order to understand more fully why wisdom was so
closely connected with healing, and the relevance that this has to
the thesis that wisdom was developed to form a bridge between
the cult-centered pre-exilic national faith and the post-exilic faith
of a Jewish diaspora, certain other facts about healing in ancient
Israel need to be kept in mind. The first of these is the quite
broad observation that the medicinal arts and a concern with
securing healing are not in any significant fashion a particular
province of wisdom elsewhere in the ancient Near East. We are
not therefore entitled to assume that wisdom generally took a
special interest in health and healing.

When we turn to the ancient orient as a broad cultural
whole we find that healing, both in Egypt and Mesopotamia,
was largely subsumed within the range of activities covered by
the cultus. There exists a large body of texts from ancient Egypt
which shows that the treatment of disease there was primarily
the responsibility of a priesthood. The guidance and ministry
that this offered consisted of prayers for restoration to health,
combined with semi-magical exorcisms to remove the spirit-

causing sickness. In addition, priests could advise on the wearing of amulets to ward off the influence of harmful powers. Because sickness was believed to have been caused either by the invasion of evil spirits, or by offenses which had aroused the divine anger, the entire process of healing was directly related to the cultus.

In Babylon, similarly, the healing art was a specialized province of the priesthood and two classes of priest were especially designated to handle such needs. The celebrated law code of Hammurabi makes special legal provisions for the careful control of the vital, but potentially dangerous, priestly ministrations leading to healing. Throughout the entire Babylonian civilization the manifestation of illness is assumed to be a religious problem and accordingly is wholly dealt with by cultic officials. Its causes are assumed to be traceable either to a person's having offended a deity, or to an attack by an evil spirit. Disease was part of a culture-awareness relating to evil spirits and powers of curse which were believed to be capable of undermining the health of a human being. The remedies proffered by the Babylonian priests were of a semi-magical character, consisting of the wearing of amulets and the utterance of numerous types of incantation to expel the invasion by the harmful spirit. In addition, the priestly ministration placed great emphasis upon a variety of forms of divination in order to make prognoses as to the cause of the illness and the hope of recovery.

When we turn to the pages of the Hebrew Bible the situation is strikingly similar. A most important point for our concern with wisdom is the recognition that, in early Israel, the diagnosis and treatment of disease were wholly in the purview and realm of responsibility of the cultus. Supremely this pointed to the work of the priest, but also the assistance of the prophet could be involved in diagnosing the causes of the problem and its probable outcome. Consistently in the earliest period the predominant assumption regarding illness was that it had been brought on by a condition of guilt. Hence, there is no very clear distinction between sin and guilt, as the translations of several psalms, and particularly of Isa 53, have been forced to recognize. Two narratives illustrate these fundamental Hebrew assumptions about illness very clearly.

The first is in Exod 15:22-26 and narrates how Moses "healed" the bitter waters at the desert spring Marah by putting into the spring the leaves of a tree which God had pointed out to him. This made the waters "sweet" (v. 25). This account is then followed by an assurance concerning the promise of healing generally:

> There the Lord made for them a statute and an ordinance and there he tested them, saying, "If you will diligently hearken to the voice of the Lord your God, and do that which is right in his eyes, and give heed to his commandments and keep all his statutes, I will put none of the diseases upon you which I put upon the Egyptians; for I am the Lord, your healer."
>
> Exod 15:25-26

Not only do we find here the affirmation, embodied into a divine title (*El-Ropheka*), that God alone gives healing, but we also encounter the explicit expression that it is this same deity who sends diseases upon people, as upon the Egyptians.

The second passage that relates directly to a concern with disease and healing is to be found in the extended account of a threatening illness which befell king Hezekiah (Isa 38). Here the ministry of the prophet Isaiah was directly involved, at first in offering a fatal diagnosis of the outcome of the affliction. Subsequently this was modified after Hezekiah responded piously towards God in accepting unwaveringly the divine verdict (Isa 38:5). Once again the assumption that pervades the narrative is that both the original disease, apparently an affliction of a boil (Isa 38:21), and the healing, came from God. The prophet primarily acted as the messenger from God to the king, and only a very modest pharmaceutical treatment is referred to (v. 21).

Clearly in early Israel three assumptions were basic to the understanding and treatment of disease. The first is that all sickness came from God. Consequently, a second assumption followed on directly from this which was that healing also could only come from God. The third assumption was that disease was inextricably bound up with experiences of sin and guilt so that sickness was primarily viewed in terms of punishment or warning from God. Illness could be described as uncleanness, and in turn uncleanness could only be countered by holiness. This point is well brought out in the affirmation which brings to a close the list of types of disease/uncleanness in Lev 13-15 where the levitical responsibility for careful diagnosis is established:

> Thus you shall keep the people of Israel separate from their uncleanness, lest they die in their uncleanness by defiling my tabernacle that is in their midst.
>
> Lev 15:31

Health is seen as a matter which relates directly to the regulations and activities of worship. Disease threatens the holiness of the sanctuary, and in turn the holiness of the sanctuary provides a means of protection against disease. This latter point is remarkably well illustrated from the symbolic imagery of Ezekiel's vision of the the reconstructed temple of Jerusalem where the holy life-giving blessing of the cultus is portrayed as a river (Ezek 47:1-12):

> And wherever the river goes every living creature which swarms will live, and there will be very many fish; for this water goes there, that the waters of the sea may become fresh; so everything will live where the river goes...And on the banks, on both sides of the river, there will grow all kinds of trees for food. Their leaves

will not wither nor their fruit fail, but they will bear fresh
fruit every month, because the water flows for them
from the sanctuary. Their fruit will be for food, and
their leaves for healing.

Ezek 47:9,12

Not only do we find here a symbolic expression of the
notion that the cultus secures the blessing of life, but this is
blended together with a recognition of the healing power of
certain herbs. From this we are made aware of the fact that, in
ancient Israel, even the apothecary's skill and expertise were
directly related to the activities of the cultus as the action of
Moses reported in Exod 15:25 shows. Ezekiel's imagery points
us to an understanding that, in early Israel, the wide range of
concepts concerning life and death, sickness and healing
essentially formed part of a single comprehensive view of life.
This was dualistic in its nature in that on one side were ranged
life, health, fertility, prosperity, holiness, honor and peace, and
against this were ranged death, disease, uncleanness, famine and
shame. The former constituted a condition of blessing and the
latter a realm of curse.

There is a particular significance therefore in the
deuteronomic legislation which describes Israel's future life as
poised between the categories of either blessing (Deut 28:1-14)
or curse (Deut 28:15-68), according to the obedience to the
Mosaic *torah* which the nation displays. Disease is viewed as
the primary means by which God manifests his wrath towards
his people:

The Lord will make the pestilence cleave to you until he
has consumed you off the land which you are entering to
take possession of it.

Deut 28:21;
cf. vv.22-24

In the formulation of the deuteronomic blessings and curses all human experience is effectively summarized as a choice between a way of "life" and a way of "death." By recognizing this primary concern of cultus with concepts of "life" and "death," we also get a glimpse of the reasoning which made the Baal cultus, with its central focus in a conflict between Baal, as the Lord and giver of life, and Mot as the god of death, so long-lasting a temptation to Israel. Life itself seemed to mirror this daily conflict which faced every human being and threatened the enjoyment of life with the ever-present possibility of death.

The diagnosis of sickness and the overcoming of this through healing were therefore part of the responsibility of the priesthood in ancient Israel. It was this priestly cultus which, by its protection of Israel's condition as a "holy" nation (cf. Deut 14:2), made it possible for the holiness of the people to be preserved. What is striking about the Deuteronomic legislation, when compared with the roughly contemporaneous levitical legislation of the Holiness Code, is that *torah*, rather than the actual praxis of the cultus, has the pre-eminent position (cf. especially Deut 4:40). Nevertheless, cult and *torah* are assumed to be in a harmonious working relationship with each other.

A further outworking of this direct relationship in early Israel between the cultus and the experience of disease is to be found in the Psalter. Many psalms were undoubtedly primarily composed as prayers for healing. Among the individual lament psalms preserved in the Psalter, therefore, are several composed for recitation by a worshipper of the Lord who had been stricken with illness. In seeking a gracious act of healing from God the ministry of a temple-servant is usually also to be inferred, and clearly often there would be a promise of making a sacrificial offering to God once the recovery had been made. What is rather alarming to the modern mind is that such psalms show how very minimal was the availability of any medical or pharmaceutical help from the cultus to assist in the process of healing. A good example of such a prayer for healing is to be found in Ps 38:

> There is no soundness in my flesh
>> because of thy indignation;
>> there is no health in my bones because of my sin.
> For my iniquities have gone over my head;
>> they weigh like a burden too heavy for me.
> My wounds grow foul and fester
>> because of my foolishness,
> I am utterly bowed down and prostrate;
>> all the day I go about mourning.
> For my loins are filled with burning,
>> and there is no soundness in my flesh.
> I am utterly spent and crushed;
>> I groan because of the tumult of my heart.
>>   Ps 38:3-8

Here we find how directly interwoven were the ideas of sin and sickness and how minimal appears to have been the degree of medical care available. However, the instance of Isa 38:21 indicates that it may be largely the nature of the biblical tradition which has left us in ignorance of the extent to which the priesthood would have made use of healing herbs.

Wisdom as the Path of Life

It is a very noteworthy feature of the wisdom tradition that it displays a marked shift in the biblical interpretation of ideas concerning life and death. The ancient dualism between these concepts, which lay at the very heart of ancient Near Eastern cultic ideas and rites, is strikingly transformed. Whereas in Canaanite religion Mot was the god of death, who appears as the arch-opponent of Baal, the god who gives life, we find in the wisdom tradition the complete de-mythologizing of death. Even in the sections of Proverbs which have a strong claim to represent the oldest stratum of Israelite wisdom teaching, we find that adherence to wisdom is affirmed to be the path to life. Conversely it is the rejection of wisdom which constitutes the way to death:

> My son, do not forget my teaching,
>   but let your heart keep my commandments;
> for length of days and years of life
>   and abundant welfare will they give you.
>   Prov 3:1-2

Even the ancient mythological image of "the tree of life" can be completely re-minted at the hands of the sages, since they can affirm of wisdom:

> She is a tree of life to those who lay hold of her;
>   those who hold her fast are called happy.
>   Prov 3:18

> In the path of right action is life,
>   but the way of error leads to death.
>   Prov 12:28

A wide-ranging series of actions demanded by the precepts of wisdom are said to lead to long life and, by implication, also a full and satisfying one. Over against this, folly and ignorance lead to death and its dreary underworld. At first this seems to be almost entirely a metaphorical use of the terminology of "life" and "death," since both concepts are heavily moralized. Wisdom is said to be a "fountain of life" :

> The teaching of the wise is a fountain of life,
>   that one may avoid the snares of death.
>   Prov 13:14;
>   cf. also 14:27

To reject the teaching of the wise is to step out on the path to ruin. In the post-exilic hortatory poems of Prov 1-9 this re-evaluation of the older life/death dualism of the cultus is even more heavily developed, since we find that the idea of "death" is consistently moralized. The pursuit of immorality is the way to death (Prov 1:32; 2:18; 5:5, etc.), and this implies not merely a condition of "God-forsakenness," but a very real warning of the probability of early death. In contrast, wisdom holds the key to well-being and long life:

> She is more precious than jewels,
>   and nothing you desire can compare with her.
> Long life is in her right hand;
>   in her left hand are riches and honor.
> Her ways are ways of pleasantness,
>   and all her paths are peace.
> She is a tree of life to those who lay hold of her;
>   those who hold her fast are called happy.
>   Prov 3:15-18

Wisdom is the open pathway to blessing and it is clearly evident that the protection and long life that the older tradition of Israel had demonstrably linked with the cultus was now being proffered through wisdom. We could explain this as a mark of the fact that the cultus and the teachers of wisdom had started from their respective beginnings with different presuppositions regarding the conceptualizing of order in the experienced world. For the cultus it was founded on notions of holiness and blessing, countering the dangers of uncleanness and guilt. For the sages, however, their assumptions about the order of the world were assumptions built upon the teaching of right dealing and a prudential looking to the consequences of actions. The similarities, however, are so striking that a more intentional, and skillfully constructed program of re-evaluation appears to be involved.

Wisdom does not simply stand aside from the cultus, offering a different interpretation of the life-death dualism that had found its strongest focal point in the cult-drama of the contest between Baal and Mot, but offers a consciously different interpretation of the way to life. What we are faced with in the proverbial teachings regarding the pursuit of wisdom as the way to life and healing can be seen to offer a clear alternative to the earlier cultic notions based on the mediation of holiness through the cultus. Wisdom's guidance regarding the overcoming of death and sickness is essentially a-cultic in its claims and interpretations, not because it opposes the cultus in an overt way, but because it seeks to reach out beyond it.

Our thesis has been that wisdom, because it was based in its origins upon a non-national and cosmic interpretation of creation and human society, could view the cultus as too restricted in its operation and proffered blessings to be adaptable to a people forced to live among other peoples, far from their original homeland. To a people cut off from the benefits of a temple cultus and priesthood, its life-saving protection had become an inaccessible means of blessing. In the very territorial basis of its assumptions concerning holiness, the entire concept of a temple and its benefits had shown themselves to be limited and increasingly irrelevant. Something more than holiness was required if Jews living in the "unclean" lands of the diaspora were to have life. The alternatives would appear to have lain between abandoning interest in the cultus of Jerusalem in favor of an alien cultus closer to hand, or seeking a different path to "life." It is this that wisdom, as developed in the teaching of the book of Proverbs, sought to offer by promising a new path to deliverance from the threat of death more truly universal in its scope than that offered by the cult.

This then is the course that post-exilic Judaism, faced with the needs of accommodating the needs of a growing multiplicity of scattered communities, followed in the way in which it developed its tradition of wisdom. Israel had lost its national structure as a community. Yet it was this very structure which had been inseparable from Israel's consciousness of being a "holy nation." Under the Persian administration of the post-exilic era there was no Jewish nation as such, but only a small central community in Jerusalem and its environs and a larger variety of dispersed Jewish settlements.

We may note how scholarship has already recognized the importance to an understanding of wisdom of the process of *spiritualizing* and *moralizing* cultic concepts. This feature, which became so significant an aspect of the later Jewish piety of the diaspora in the New Testament era, has been traced back to the *sapientalizing* of cultic concepts. Certainly there are clear indications that both sacrifice and prayer are strikingly moralized in the way in which the teachers of wisdom handle them. God "hears" the prayers of the righteous, but is far from the wicked. (Prov 15:29).

Although it is clear that the sages, both of ancient Israel and of the surrounding nations, say little about the cultus, there is no marked evidence that they displayed any consistent antipathy to it and its proffered way to blessing. At the most they either took it for granted as a part of life, or they tacitly ignored it in favor of their own more immediate, and frequently more individual, concerns.

Yet it becomes clear from the way in which the teachers of wisdom presented assurances that overlapped with those that were proffered by the cultus, that their teaching now preserved in the book of Proverbs displays a strong awareness of these cultic promises of securing "life" through the pursuit of holiness. We have argued, in examining the sages' affirmations regarding "the fear of the Lord," that their very indifference towards the concept of holiness is a studied indifference. Instead of supporting and encouraging the preservation of holiness, they have consciously replaced such a notion by what they regarded as a more psychologically relevant concept.

In setting aside, and seeking to replace, the idea of cultic holiness by that of "the fear of the Lord," the wisdom teachers, however, left a particular gap that needed to be filled in regard to ideas of health and healing. Since holiness was closely akin to "purity," and the ignoring of the prescriptions of holiness an open threat of "uncleanness," it became vital that health and healing too should come under the purview of wisdom.

The Significance of Sickness and Healing in Post-exilic Wisdom

Before looking at what wisdom has to say about sickness and healing, it is important to note the significance of a narrative tradition that belongs to the post-exilic age, but which stands outside of the wisdom tradition. This is to be found in 2 Chr 16:11 and refers to a sickness which befell king Asa. We should bear in mind the narrative of Isa 38 which brings to our attention the way in which Hezekiah's response to illness was shown to be a major indication of his piety and faithfulness to Yahweh. The converse is true in respect of Asa:

> In the thirty-ninth year of his reign Asa was diseased in his feet, and his disease became severe; yet even in his disease he did not seek the Lord, but sought help from physicians.
>
> 2 Chr 16:11

Sickness was a test of faith, or more narrowly a test of loyalty, and the increased interest in the subject of sickness in the Chronicler's work, when compared with that of the Deuteronomistic Historian, indicates a feature of post-exilic Jewish life. It is not that sickness has become more common than before, but that there now is mentioned for the first time in the Hebrew Bible a class of physicians. The priestly monopoly in caring for sickness and seeking health and healing is no longer complete. Probably it never was a monopoly and there always had existed other practitioners of medicine, specialists in breaking spells and overcoming powerful forms of magic which formed an ever-present alternative to the spartan aid of the official cultus. Such would have been the strange women mentioned in Ezek 13:17-23 who sewed magic bands upon all wrists, and made veils for the heads of persons of every stature, in the hunt for souls (Ezek 17:18). As in so many communities, both ancient and modern, and as Christian missionaries have repeatedly encountered in many countries, there exists in the world many differing styles and traditions of medicine. So often it is the magical, or semi-magical, which claims to offer the greatest potency and assurance of recovery. At the same time, resort to such avenues of healing usually carries with it the stigma of disloyalty to the official faith of the community, and sometimes the very negative threat of having resorted to dangerous, and potentially evil, power.

Our contention is that it was precisely this consciousness of the non-Yahwistic and "pagan" alternatives to the traditional cult-centeredness of Israel's tradition of health and healing which gave rise to the sages' special preoccupation with the theme. No doubt there existed an established tradition that the preservation of life through medicine and healing, together with the identification healing herbs, formed a part of the mysterious order of the world which formed wisdom's primary assumption. As a consequence, adherence to the teachings of wisdom and "the fear of the Lord" could maintain the traditional loyalty of Israel's inherited faith, but extend the promise of life and healing far beyond the frontiers of the older cult-orientation of holiness and purity. Our argument is that it was in the post-exilic situation, where a growing number of Jews were compelled to live outside the scope of the Jerusalem cultus and its ministry, that this feature of wisdom took on a special importance. As a consequence it has come to receive a very marked degree of attention in the preserved tradition of the book of Proverbs.

It is useful to note the prominence which is attached to the claim that adherence to wisdom can promote a long life and that this marks a central feature of the life of a person who "fears the Lord":

> The Fear of Yahweh is the beginning of wisdom,
>   and the knowledge of the Holy One is insight.
> For by me your days will be multiplied,
>   and years will be added to your life.
> If you are wise, you are wise for yourself;
>   if you scoff, you alone will bear it.
>   Prov 9:10-12

Just as the idea of "the fear of the Lord" represents the primary way in which wisdom has endeavored to extend the earlier notion of holiness in a more spiritual, and less physical, direction, so also was it important to stress that the path of wisdom led to health and long life. The fruit of the wise and God-fearing way of life was that life itself should be long:

> The fruit of the righteous is a tree of life,
>   but lawlessness takes away lives.
>   Prov 11:30

In keeping with such an assurance, the notion of "death" is stripped of all its quasi-mythological and divinized features and becomes inseparable from morality (cf. Prov 7:27, 9:18, etc.).

The section in Prov 9:10-12 appears designed to serve as a summarizing conclusion to the teaching of chapters 1-9 and presents an overall conclusion about the benefits and goals of wisdom. Similarly in Prov 3:1-2 we have a broad survey of what it is that wisdom offers those who seek her:

> My son, do not forget my teaching,
>   but let your heart keep my commandments;
> for length of days and years of life
>   and abundant welfare will they give you.
> Let not loyalty and faithfulness forsake you;
>   bind them about your neck,
>   write them on the tablet of your heart.

It will be healing to your flesh
    and refreshment to your bones.

Long life is in her right hand;
    in her left hand are riches and honor,

She is a tree of life to those who lay hold of her;
    those who hold her fast are called happy.

My son, be attentive to my words;
    incline your ear to my sayings.
Let them not escape from your sight;
    keep them within your heart.
For they are life to him who finds them,
    and healing to all his flesh.

                        Prov 3:1-3,8, 16,18;
                        4:20-22

When we come to examine the older wisdom that is contained in Prov 10-25 we find that the themes of a long life and of healing are present, but scarcely with the same degree of prominence that is accorded to them in Prov 1-9. What appears to have taken place is that, as in the case of the idea of "the fear of Yahweh," the scribes who have shaped the tradition of wisdom in the post-exilic era have done so with a strong consciousness of the needs of a diaspora community. The very internationalism and a-cultic features of wisdom have made it into an excellent vehicle for developing and extending the claims of loyalty to Yahweh beyond the scope of the cultus. The older cultic *torah* has been enlarged into a compendium of wide-ranging instructions which present the way of wisdom as the way to a long and healthy life. What the earlier laws of Deuteronomy and the Holiness Code had promised as the benefits of loyal participation in the cult of Yahweh are now presented as more universally available to those "who fear Yahweh." A piety centered on the cult has become a pious way of life which is not indifferent to the cultus, but which is no longer dependent on it. Wisdom has proved itself able to control and protect those areas of life which the older holiness, based on the temple cultus, could no longer reach.

At first this can appear as a kind of "secularizing" and "de-sanctifying" of life, and it could appear that this was part of the inevitable consequence of the impact of wisdom upon human thinking. To a modest degree this may be true, but in general it needs to be argued that this was very far from being a "secular" movement of thought in anything like the manner that such a term would convey in the modern world. Rather it was a powerful attempt to use the tradition of wisdom, which had authentic Israelite roots in the Jerusalem court, and to a lesser extent in the national life more broadly, in order to build up a new type of instructional vehicle.

So far as a distinctive concern with health and healing is concerned it is especially worthy of note that the older proverbial wisdom displays a very strong consciousness that health involves a strong element of psychological well-being. The very roots of wisdom's understanding of health are traced to a healthy frame of mind:

> A cheerful heart is good medicine,
>> but a downcast spirit dries up the bones.
>>>> Prov 17:22

Similarly there are ways of using speaking which lead to healing (Prov 12:18), where it is possible that the assertion is meant metaphorically of the healing of relationships (cf. also Prov 16:24). Yet even with such an interpretation the implication is that stressful relationships are destructive of well-being, whereas positive and happy relationships are vitally important for health. This sense of the importance of health and healing in human relationships is found expressed in Prov 13:17:

A bad messenger plunges men into trouble,
but a faithful envoy brings healing.
                                        Prov 13:17

The central importance of a healthy disposition of mind in
maintaining health is also affirmed by the instruction of Prov
14:30:

A tranquil mind gives life to the flesh,
but passion makes the bones rot.

We should certainly draw attention in this connection to
the sharp criticism of the noisy and quarrelsome wife who could
be destructive of the entire household. Perhaps most striking of
all in this regard, in view of modern awareness of the destructive
impact of stress upon human health and relationships, is the
instruction to be found in Prov 18:14:

A man's spirit will endure sickness;
but a broken spirit who can bear?

The idea of a "broken spirit" here seems to point to some
condition of deep depression. There can be no doubting that the
plain sense of such a saying is that long-term psychological
stress is more damaging to health than a temporary affliction.
Overall our contention has been that, in its special concern with
ideas of health and healing, and in the avoidance of death, the
teaching of wisdom has been developed in Israel in a distinctive
direction. It has taken on a special concern precisely at the point
where the ministry of the cultus could no longer effectively
reach. So far as we can see, pre-exilic Israelite life was marked
by an attitude to disease and healing which viewed it wholly as
falling within the purview of the cultus. Sickness was a form of
uncleanness and belonged within the overall categories of sin
and guilt. The priest was the practitioner of health and healing.
To look outside the priestly realm, in order to seek healing and

deliverance from the grip of disease, as clearly many were tempted to do, was viewed in the strongest terms as a straying from loyalty to Yahweh. Yet, after the catastrophes of 598 and 587 BCE, many former citizens of Judah found themselves compelled to live in a situation where the sanctifying and restorative power of the cultus could no longer be readily accessible.

Nevertheless, clearly men and women fell victim to illness and disease as much in an alien "unclean" land as they had previously done in the territory of Judah. So wisdom came to develop a wide-ranging concern with ideas of health and healing as a part of the wise order of life which God had created for his creatures. A non-cultic approach to the problems of sickness and healing came to be developed which no longer carried the stigma of "disloyalty" which was still capable of being levelled against king Asa by the Chronicler. Medicine came to be viewed as part of the science of "life," available to all who displayed a proper fear of the Lord. So it came about that, as this tradition received yet stronger impulses from the Greek spirit in the second century BCE, Ben Sira could argue his case for a wholly independent practice of medicine, totally outside the cultus. Similarly the pharmacist too, with his knowledge of healing plants and herbs, needed no longer to be a Levite like Moses, or a prophet like Elijah. It was a distinct ministry which, like that of the medical practitioner, was a gift of God.

To call this development "secular," which we find in Ben Sira and which has thereafter come down to us as a foundation for our modern ideas of medicine, would be mistaken. It is true that it is presented as "non-cultic," but it is so emphatically stressed as a gift of God himself, that it too, like the ministry of priesthood, is seen to belong to the beneficent divine governance of the world. It was the ways of this divine governance that the zealous sages of ancient Judaism sought to explore.

CHAPTER THREE

WISDOM AND THE ROYAL COURT

There are a significant number of sayings in the book of Proverbs which deal with the king and which present him in an extremely positive and favorable light. This is striking in view of the fact that in the prophetic literature generally, and in the narrative literature of 1&2 Samuel and 1&2 Kings, a far more guarded and often downright critical attitude towards the monarchy is maintained. The collections of Psalms and Proverbs display a strongly pro-monarchic tendency, whereas the historical and prophetic literature of the Old Testament is quite consistently critical of kingship as an institution.

This situation is particularly noteworthy because it has long been recognized by scholars that psalm-writing and the collection of didactic wisdom sayings reached far back into the period of the monarchy. Yet we have to keep in mind the fact that, in spite of the early composition of many wisdom sayings, it is evident that the editing of the book of Proverbs was predominantly a post-exilic literary task. There is a close parallel here with the Psalter since, in spite of the early origin of many of the individual psalms, the collection of the Psalter as a whole was undertaken in the post-exilic era. Inevitably this major shift in the historical and liturgical context in which the psalms were used carried with it some significant shifts in their interpretation.

Similarly with the teaching of the wise, it seems evident that instructions which originated in the pre-exilic era, were retained and re-interpreted in the new setting provided by the situation after 587 BCE.

Recent attention has been given to the question of the significance of the retention of royal psalms in the post-exilic era when Israel had no reigning king. The potential eschatological-messianic implications of this preservation cannot be ignored. When we come to ask why Judaism retained its royal wisdom in an age when it had no king, it seems unlikely that an explanation can be found in terms of messianic eschatology.

The King as Exemplary Wise Man

It is certainly not difficult to recognize how, and for what purposes Israel's scribes of the monarchic era composed, collected and preserved didactic sentence instruction concerning the role of the king. What is more obscure, and yet in many respects far more interesting, is why this royal sentence instruction remained important to later generations of Jews. Much discussion has focused on the question of the extent to which the collection and promotion of wisdom in early Israel was an activity of the royal court. Although it is easily possible to exaggerate the extent of this, there are numerous indications that this was the case. We encounter several lines of evidence which show that, in the early period, Israel's wisdom tradition was centrally focused upon the figure of the king and the state administration of which he was the head. This finds further support from the recognition that, in its origins, the collection and dissemination of wisdom in Israel was significantly influenced from Egypt where the court was a central focus of *ma'at*. That some of the content of wisdom teaching was directly associated with the skills of counsel and government appropriate to a royal court further supports such a contention. Although it would be pressing the case too far to regard wisdom in the pre-exilic period as an activity exclusively promoted within the royal court, it would certainly appear that this was primarily the sphere where the virtues of wisdom were most sought after.

That there existed a tradition of folk-wisdom, as the rhetorical and imaginative expertise of the wise woman from Tekoa illustrates (2 Sam 14:2), is evident; and there are further features of preserved wisdom teaching which reveal its concern with farmers and smallholders, indicating that it related to a wide social area and not simply that of the court. Those who are addressed in several of the admonitions are clearly assumed to possess wealth, as well as both the leisure and the incentive to pursue the cultured acquisition of wisdom. Yet even such a relatively wealthy rural landowning class must have had close links with the royal court. Overall, therefore, it is not difficult to see that there were strong factors in Israel's wisdom which point to the royal court as both a focal center for the collection and acquisition of wisdom, as well as a pivotal social institution for all that the teaching of it assumed about social order and justice. In speaking of the court-orientation of wisdom, therefore, we are concerned to affirm that the royal court is presumed upon as the structural center of the social realm.

What we must not do is to fall into the trap of making the assumption that wisdom, because it was nurtured in the court, was necessarily primarily addressed to those who were active at court and who were directly occupied with some function within the royal administration. Clearly sometimes this was the case, as certain proverbial instructional sayings show (cf. Prov 23:1-5), but this would not, and could not, always have been so. What is at issue in the recognition of the close relationship between the promotion of wisdom and the institution of kingship in Israel's pre-exilic period is the awareness that wisdom presupposed a monarch. As a consequence, the assumptions of wisdom concerning virtue, piety and social obligation were such as to presuppose the pivotal role of the king as the legitimate authority within the social realm. As a consequence the wise man was assumed to be a loyal citizen who paid his taxes and respected the officers of the king. Sometimes, but not necessarily always, he may himself have been an official of the royal court.

The argument that I am concerned with regarding this close connection between wisdom and monarchy in the pre-exilic development of Israel is that, hitherto, in examining the instructions and admonitions relating to the king, far too much attention has been given to what wisdom has to say about the royal person as an individual. At the same time there has been far too little concern with the understanding of the office that he represented. In large measure the king, as portrayed in wisdom instruction, is throughout a fictive and highly artificial figure. It is, however, not his own individual personality that mattered to the wisdom teachers, but rather the office that he represented. They scarcely presumed to be offering the king advice as to his own personal conduct. We clearly misinterpret such teaching, therefore, if we try to understand it as though it were seeking to convey a character description of any specific individual, or as though it were aimed, rather obsequiously, at flattering the king. Once we abandon any attempt to understand the wisdom sayings concerning the kingship in this fashion, then they take on a much more interesting and convincing significance as an exposition of the intellectual assumptions and aims of the political structure of Israelite society. Furthermore it also becomes far more intelligible why royal wisdom remained of great importance to Jewish society after the demise of the monarchy in 587 BCE.

In order to understand the significance of this we need to recognize that, in the post-exilic period, the institution of kingship, and the state of which the king was the representative head, survived for Judaism only in a much modified form. No longer was there a king sitting on the throne of David in Jerusalem whose appointment could be understood in terms of a divine dynastic covenant made at a foundational moment of Israel's history. Instead the king was a foreigner whom the majority of Jews, whether they lived in Judah and Jerusalem or further afield, were hardly ever likely to see. His authority therefore was mediated through his representatives, some of them foreigners and some of them Jews, and could not be legitimated in terms of Jewish history in the strictest sense. In contrast to this the traditional "nationalist" form of Israel's political theology had been rooted in the affirmation of the covenant between God and the house of David which could only survive in the post-exilic era as part of an eschatological hope.

However there existed in the inherited tradition of Israelite wisdom a different, but significantly impressive understanding of the foundations of socio-political order which focused upon the nature and authority of the king. In this, the divine wisdom was believed to be manifested in, and mediated to, the larger realm of society through the monarch. It is the framework of this wisdom tradition, which we find still preserved in the book of Proverbs. After the downfall of the native Israelite monarchy, the tradition of royal wisdom nevertheless survived to form a major part of Jewish intellectual restructuring in the changed political situation of the post-exilic age. For the Judaism of this transformed political world the retention of royal wisdom became particularly important since it vested the concept of the king's authority in the divine order of creation and no longer in the national historical tradition of Israel.

We can look then at certain of the sentence instruction that points to the importance of the kingship, recognizing that such teaching originated in a pre-exilic setting, but has retained its significance in this wider post-exilic context:

Oracular decisions are on the lips of a king;
  his mouth does not err in giving judgment
                                    Prov 16:10

A little later in the same chapter a series of sayings extol even more forcibly the role of the king as the upholder of justice

and virtue in society. These present the royal office as a source
of great good for the entire community:

> It is an abomination for kings to do evil,
>   for the throne is established by right action.
> Truthful lips are the delight of a king,
>   and he loves one who speaks what is true.
> A king's anger is a messenger of death,
>   and a wise person will appease it.
> In the expression of a king's face there is life,
>   and his favour is like the clouds
>   that bring the spring rain.
>
> Prov 16:12-15

We can compare also the saying:

> My son, fear the Lord and the king,
>   and do not disobey either of them;
> for disaster from them will rise suddenly,
>   and who knows the ruin that
>   will come from them both?
>
> Prov 24:21-22

It is striking that this piece of sentence instruction
directly equates respect for God with respect for the king on the
grounds that both possess the power to bring ruin to those who
oppose them. This special interest in the idea of the "wrath" of
the king appears at first to suggest that kings were particularly
bad-tempered and irascible personalities. Whether or not this
was the case, it is certainly not this kind of character assessment
that is the purpose of the wisdom instruction. Rather it is that
the king represents political power, and the notion of the royal
"wrath" serves to pictorialize and embody the concept of the
power to inflict retributive justice through the king, who stands
as the head of state:

A king's wrath is like the growling of a lion,
    but his favor is like dew upon the grass.
Prov 19:12

In a rather similar vein the king's ability to search out
and punish misdemeanors is presented as being absolute:

A king who sits on the throne of judgment
    winnows all evil with his eyes.
Prov 20:8

A wise king winnows the wicked,
    and drives the wheel over them.
Prov 20:26

It seems highly likely that the unique ability of the king to search
out hidden things, which is also affirmed by the teaching of the
sages, was intended to be especially understood in regard to the
royal ability to root out felons and criminals:

It is the glory of God to conceal things,
    but the glory of kings is to search things out.
Prov 25:2

Further sayings concerning the role of the king in society
are to be found in Prov 14:28; 20:28; 21:1; 25:3, 5. Essentially
we may regard such teaching as part of the concern of the wise
to uphold the political and legal authority of the monarchy. Such
sayings relate primarily to the royal office, rather than to the
personal character of the ruler. Certainly we should not suppose
that this teaching was aimed directly at the king, admonishing
him to be a just and upright ruler. It is more or less taken for
granted that he will be, since it belongs to the kingly office that
he should uphold the authority and virtues of wisdom.

    At the same time we may note that the sages were
sufficiently cognizant of the potential for tyranny and misrule

that belonged to the royal office to include sayings concerning
cruel and oppressive rulers in their range of teaching:

> Like a roaring lion or a charging bear
>> is a wicked ruler over a poor people.
> A ruler who lacks understanding is a cruel oppressor;
>> but he who hates unjust gain will prolong his days.
>> Prov 28:15-16

From the title employed it seems highly likely that such sayings
were not so much aimed at the kingly person per se, but rather at
those many subordinate officials, whose greed and oppressive-
ness were almost legendary in antiquity. This would appear to
be the intention that lies behind the saying:

> When the righteous are in authority, the people rejoice;
>> but when the wicked rule, the people groan
>> Prov 29:2

Certainly the teaching of Qoheleth (Ecclesiastes) points
us in the direction of affirming the basic principle that kingship
is a necessary office of the state to prevent anarchy, even though
there existed beneath the throne a host of minor officials whose
greedy and disreputable behavior put in question the basic
understanding that the throne was built on wisdom and
righteousness:

> If you see in a province the poor oppressed and justice
> and right violently taken away, do not be amazed at the
> matter; for the high official is watched by a higher, and
> there are yet higher ones over them. But in all a king is
> an advantage to a land with cultivated fields.
>> Eccl 5:8-9;
>> cf. Eccl 4:13-16

The saying in Prov 16:10 is striking because of the high profile that it gives to the king as the administrator of justice. Commentators have noted that the claim that the king can make judgements comparable to those of a priestly oracle compares directly with the skill attributed to Ahithophel in 2 Sam 16:23. It similarly links directly with the ascription to Solomon of great insight in reaching legal verdicts over the case of the child claimed by two mothers (1 Kgs 3:16-28).

We can recognize from our knowledge of the actual administrative organization of royal courts in ancient times that the king's role in legal affairs was largely carried out through qualified officials. He stood simply as the figurehead for the authority of the state to administer all juridical affairs and it is this feature which has motivated wisdom's pointing to the king as the embodiment and symbolic representative of justice. So far as wisdom was concerned this was a central, and wholly vital aspect of the king's concern to maintain authority within the kingdom that he ruled. Control of the administration of law was the foundational platform by which the king retained political power in his own hands.

We have noted that, in antiquity as in the present, there were professional legal experts who handled such matters, even though the king accepted ultimate responsibility for their work. This piece of sentence instruction therefore deals with the king only in a purely fictive manner. It testifies to the integration of wisdom with the notion of legal authority and it vests all such legal authority in the state. Strikingly too, it achieves this by comparing such legal pronouncements with the ultimate, and unquestionable, authority of a divine oracle. By doing this, it appears consciously to be setting aside the use of manipulative, and semi-magical, means of determining difficult legal cases such as priests employed. We may compare the arrangements stipulated in Deut 16:18-20; 17:8-13 where only very difficult cases are left for the priests to handle. This major saying concerning royal wisdom, therefore, places the royal office at the highest level of authority in legal matters, and appears designed to push aside older religious forms of legal decision-making. Taken overall we can see that, for the authors of these proverbial pieces of sentence instruction, the fundamental assumption that pervades them is that put into the mouth of personified wisdom:

> By me kings reign, and rulers decree what is just;
> by me princes rule, and nobles govern the earth.
> Prov 8:15-16

The situation is not fundamentally different with the other royal sayings that we have noted. The saying of Prov 16:12 extolling the virtues of the king appears incredible in a strictly historical sense, but wholly appropriate and justified in the context of a philosophy of the state:

> It is an abomination to kings to do evil,
> for the throne is established by righteousness.
> Prov 16:12

The king is the pivotal center of justice, so that he is, by definition, righteous on account of the office he holds. A central feature of the royal wisdom that we are concerned with therefore is the way in which it integrates the concept of wisdom with political authority.

What we can reconstruct of the intellectual assumptions of such wisdom teaching is that, by focusing upon the figure of the king as the center, wisdom could assert that the social and moral realms interlocked with that of creation itself. Moral and political order were part of the order of creation.

When at least some of the proverbial teaching that we have mentioned first originated, it seems probable that the king that was referred to would have been a native Israelite ruler, undoubtedly of the dynasty of David. However, once this political state of affairs no longer prevailed after 587 BCE, then it certainly did not mean that the understanding of social and political order to which it testified was no longer necessary. In many ways such an understanding had become even more necessary since the cultic institutions and their accompanying royal mythology were no longer available and defensible in their original sense. Wisdom took over where the elaborate royal cult-mythology of the Psalms could no longer survive, except as part of an eschatological hope.

So we find that the world that is portrayed by wisdom is one in which the structures and values of society are vested in a world order which is believed to have been established at creation by God. In consequence, the situation which Israel encountered in the post-exilic period, even though it lacked a reigning Israelite monarch of the dynasty of David, nevertheless presupposed that a king held office, and ruled justly, as part of the created order of society. This was understood to be a necessary part of the divine scheme of things. Far from Israel's new political situation, where it was divided between a small community in Judah and a more scattered miscellany of communities living throughout the Persian Empire, having no place for a king, such a figure still remained essential within the horizons of wisdom. Since no one bearing the title of king had been restored to the throne in Jerusalem, it was necessary to think of the wider kingly order which was provided under the Persian imperial umbrella.

In order to appreciate the reasons why wisdom's concern with kingship and a royal court remained significant in an age when Israel itself had no king, it is valuable to reflect back upon the nature of political authority. Max Weber distinguished three major, or "ideal," types of such authority, the charismatic, the traditional and the rational, or legal. A great wealth of attention has been devoted to the nature of charismatic authority in ancient Israel. Certainly Israel's narrative history asserts very forcefully that David acquired his position as founder of the royal dynasty through the *charisma* of his own personality.

Significantly the evidence that is presented, both in the royal psalms and the prophets, for the establishing of a *traditional* basis of kingly authority through the dynasty of David was bolstered by appeal to David's charismatic excellence. Only in the broadest terms do the royal psalms and their prophetic counterparts offer anything that can be described as a rational basis for the institution of monarchy and its power. The language that is used simply affirms that God has "chosen" the royal house of David to provide Israel's line of kings. Further claim to the king's ability to administer the kingdom on God's behalf is made in terms of the mythology of divine "sonship."

These assumptions are basically cultic assumptions concerning the role of the king as a source of vitality and blessing for the nation. Yet what we find being expressed through those surviving elements of the teaching of the wise which deal with the office of the monarch is an attempt to marry the charismatic role of the king with a rational one. We have already noted that the picture that is given of the king is highly artificial and idealized. It is in no way a portrait drawn from life! Yet neither is it an expression of an obsequious court flattery. Rather it expresses convictions about the *order* of society in which both wisdom and monarchy had vital roles to play.

It is a matter of noteworthy interest therefore that, when we turn to the biblical records of the restoration in the late sixth and early fifth centuries BCE, the whole character of reporting the leadership differs from that which characterized the accounts of the founding of the monarchy. Now all interest focuses upon the offices that such figures as Zerubbabel, Ezra, and Nehemiah occupy. The roles of "governor" and "secretary," and Nehemiah's appointment as a "special commissioner" are all carefully recorded, if never completely definable. They are not charismatic figures any more in the manner of David or Solomon. Seen in the perspective of Weber's classification of types of authority the charismatic and traditional (dynastic), have wholly given way to the rational and the legal.

Solomon as the Ideal Wise King

The place where we encounter a presentation of royal wisdom in a very significant way before the final collapse of the old kingdom of Judah is to be found in the presentation of Solomon. He appears as the exemplary figure of the wise king. The origins of this tradition regarding Solomon's wisdom have been extensively discussed, and I have offered elsewhere my own evaluation of it. What is noteworthy is that the primary features of such a presentation concern those two aspects of royal wisdom that stand in the forefront of the broader interest in the connection between wisdom and the royal court. The king is put forward as the unrivaled possessor of insight into legal affairs and legal administration (cf. 1 Kgs 3:15-28). Secondly, he is portrayed as the expert administrator of trade and commercial enterprise, so that he is deservedly a supremely wealthy person (1 Kgs 10:1-25). The overall assessment of Solomon's achievement is summed up in a most convenient fashion to illustrate the way in which wisdom is seen as the foundation of wealth and prosperity:

Thus King Solomon excelled all the kings of the earth in riches and in wisdom. And the whole earth sought the presence of Solomon to hear his wisdom, which God had put into his mind.

1 Kgs 10:23-24

There may well have been some quite basic elements of the history and tradition of Solomon's reign which lent some veracity to the reputation that is afforded him concerning his wisdom. However, whatever that may have been, there can be little doubt that it is primarily the Deuteronomistic Historian who has built up and elaborated this tradition to suit a primary purpose of his own. This arose out of his evident desire to make the figure of Solomon and his reign palatable to an Israel that that rightly retained very bitter and disagreeable memories of it. The reason for doing this is clear: it was Solomon's excesses that forced the majority of Israel to withdraw their allegiance from the royal house of David. The cry of "all Israel," apart from the tribe of Judah is explicitly clear:

> What portion have we in David? We have no inheritance
> in the son of Jesse. To your tents, O Israel! Look now to
> your own house, David.
>
> 1 Kgs 12:16

Writing at a much later age, when the subsequent history of the divided kingdoms had brought only increasing weakness and decline, the Deuteronomistic Historian felt amply justified in affirming that this defection from David and his dynasty had been a tragic mistake. God acted in history "for (his) own sake and for the sake of his servant David" (2 Kgs 19:34).

So this historian has made use of popular stories about a wise king which he has applied directly and personally to the figure of Solomon. These stories relate to fitness for legal administration and the ability to create prosperity because these are the very virtues that are felt most to befit a wise king! All of this has been done in order to sustain the principle of dynastic kingship vested in the royal house of David. Seen in the light of Weber's categories, the *charismatic* excellence of David is made to support the claim of the Davidic royal house to enjoy the *traditional* authority of a monarchic dynasty. Overall the interests of the historian in 1 Kings lie in his deep commitment to this principle of traditional authority vested in a royal dynasty.

A very much changed situation confronts us when we look at the way the Chronicler presents the royal person of Solomon (1 Chr 28:1—2 Chr 9:31). Gone completely are the efforts to defend the divine validity of Solomon's succession to David, over against the rival, and certainly more conventionally legitimate, succession of Adonijah. The whole question of Solomon's right to succeed his father is hastened over in an arbitrary fashion as an issue not in dispute. David says:

And of all my sons (for the Lord has given me many sons) he has chosen Solomon my son to sit upon the throne of the kingdom of the Lord over Israel. He said to me, "It is Solomon your son who shall build my house and my courts, for I have chosen him to be my son, and I will be his father."

1 Chr 28:5-6

The succession of Solomon then follows as a matter of course. Nevertheless the next feature of the tradition that is given prominence is Solomon's dream in which he asks God for wisdom above all other gifts (2 Chr 1:7-13). He is then assured of receiving this most kingly virtue, and the wealth and prosperity that it was believed it could bring:

God answered Solomon, "Because this was in your heart, and you have not asked possessions, wealth, honor, or the life of those who hate you, and have not even asked long life, but have asked wisdom and knowledge for yourself that you may rule my people over whom I have made you king, wisdom and knowledge are granted to you I will also give you riches, possessions and honor, such as none of the kings had who were before you, and none after you shall have the like."

2 Chr 1:11-12

The tradition of Solomon's great wisdom remains of importance, but no longer in support of the contention that mattered most to the Deuteronomist that Solomon was the true dynastic heir to David. It is rather that wisdom is necessary for a worthy king, and the truly wise king will bring great prosperity and well-being to his people. As the wisest of kings, Solomon is therefore reputed also to have been the richest and most honored of all that ever were.

What we see here is that the reasoning that underlies the whole presentation is thinking in terms of Weber's third principle of authority—that of a rational and legitimate ruler. Wisdom itself has become the supreme quality that justifies Solomon's elevation to kingship. Our contention is that this is of great importance, not simply because it can explain some of the interesting historiographic procedures of the Chronicler. Rather it is that it serves excellently to illustrate how the older connection between wisdom and the royal court has been retained in the post-exilic situation. This connection between wisdom and the king enabled Judaism in the Persian era to accommodate to the idea of the divine right to rule of one who was an alien, non-Israelite and non-Yahwistic ruler. Cosmic order, as taught in the tradition of wisdom, supported the principle of kingship, even that of a foreign ruler such as Cyrus (cf. Isa 45:1; Ezra 1:1)!

It is in this context that we can discern how the inherited tradition of Solomon as the supremely wise ruler served to strengthen the claims of wisdom's "royal court ideology." Then following from this we can see in the differences in the treatment of this king in the books of Kings and Chronicles how this ideology served to assist Judaism's accommodation to the new political order which it faced in the post-exilic restoration.

Wisdom and Kingship in a Gentile Setting

There are several major ways in which the development of this royal court orientation of wisdom has served to facilitate the social development of Judaism. Most prominent among these must be placed the gradual assimilation of wisdom to the concept of *torah*. Not only does *torah* become a form of wisdom, but wisdom acquires a much higher status as part of the authorized teaching of the community. We are presented with the most striking instance of this coalescence of wisdom and *torah* in the often cited passage from Ben Sira in which he bridges the gulf between law (*torah*) as the distinctive ethnic and religious tradition of the heirs of Jacob and its function as the ordering principle of all creation which properly belongs to wisdom:

> Then the Creator of all things gave me a commandment, and the one who created me assigned a place for my tent. And he said, "Make your dwelling in Jacob, and in Israel receive your inheritance." From eternity, in the beginning, he created me, and for eternity I shall not cease to exist.
>
> Sir 24:8-9

We can note here the skilful way in which *torah* is presented as, by its essential nature, an expression of the created order of the world and of society. Already earlier we find in Deut 4:6 an initial assimilation of wisdom to *torah:*

> Behold I have taught you statutes and ordinances, ... Keep them and do them; for that will be your wisdom and your understanding in the sight of the peoples, who, when they hear all these statutes, will say,...
>
> Deut 4:5-6

However, in this passage there has clearly not yet entered into the drawing together of the two concepts the properly cosmic scope of wisdom. Instead there remains a very explicit declaration that such a *torah* is a purely national law:

> And what great nation is there, that has statutes and ordinances so righteous as all this law which I set before you this day?
>
> Deut 4:8

It is when we look carefully at recent studies of the work of Ezra and the nature of his law-book that we can see a more fundamental aspect of the way in which the very concept of *torah* is undergoing a change to give it a more universal character. This comes to the fore in the account of the commission that is entrusted to Ezra by the Persian king Artaxerxes:

> And you, Ezra, according to the wisdom of your God which is in your hand, appoint magistrates and judges who may judge all the people in the province. Beyond the River, all such as know the laws of your God; and those who do not know them, you shall teach. Whoever will not obey the law of your God and the law of the king, let judgment be strictly executed upon him, whether for death or for banishment or for confiscation of his goods or for imprisonment.
>
> Ezra 7:25-26

The terms by which the law is defined here are extremely informative. In the first place a quite explicit reference is made to the fact that the laws are to be made "according to the wisdom of your God which is in your hand." Then an indication is made that such a series of laws are to be in accord with "the law of your God." At the same time these laws are also designated "the law of your king," by which the Persian ruler is undoubtedly meant. There are in a theoretical sense two laws—a national "Jewish" law, although there is now no true Jewish nation, and also an international "Persian" law. However, clearly from Ezra's own position as Secretary for Jewish Affairs and from the law book which he subsequently read to the community in Jerusalem (Neh 8:1-8), there is a single law scroll which is designed to regulate legal affairs in the province Beyond the River, but which is to be in accord with what is approved by the Persian ruler. Law is being forced to become a more complex and flexible instrument if it is to be workable within the political situation that had emerged. No longer can it be purely "the law of the land," but it must conform to a more universal set of requirements established by the Persian government. It is also a matter of special interest to find that it is not a *torah* in any narrow, and exclusively cultic, sense of that term, since it is designed to administer matters of major crime including capital offenses.

Our contention is that it was precisely the possibility of founding such a basis of law on the principle of wisdom that made this more flexible and international form of law possible. The agency that has mediated this development is that of the kingship. As the supreme lawmaker in ancient Israel the king had been the supremely wise ruler. To that extent the principle of kingship could be adapted to respect the position of a foreign imperial ruler. Law too, as an expression of wisdom, could then be presented as a matter of more than purely national concern, and as not exclusive to one religious community.

The law that Ezra was commissioned to administer was applicable to the province of Beyond the River, which included Judah and Jerusalem. However, it is not at all difficult to see that such a concept of law which was both religiously acceptable, traditionally reputable, and which could also find approval as an expression of "the law of the king" in the Persian Empire, was vital to the survival of Judaism in the new world of the dispersion. We have only to reflect on the great difficulty which European society experienced, right down until the beginning of the nineteenth century and even beyond this, in establishing legal systems which were not oppressive to religious minorities. The fusion of the concepts of law and wisdom, which Ben Sira expresses so emphatically, appears to represent a development which must have held a foremost position in making it possible for a Jewish self-identity to maintain itself in the post-exilic world of the diaspora. Our contention is that it was the mediating position of the royal court, in which the king was regarded as both principle lawmaker and supremely wise administrator, that made this assimilation possible. Through its presentation of the king as an expression of the wise order of creation, wisdom laid the foundations for a

concept of law that was more than national and more than
territorial.

The second way in which wisdom served, in the face of
the pressures of the post-exilic age, to make a substantial
contribution to Jewish life, lay in its ability to combine ideas of
divine providence, conceived in a purely national setting, with
ideas of a just international social order. We find in the
composite history of the books of 1&2 Samuel and 1&2 Kings a
very varied series of narrative pictures of divine providence.
What is so striking is that, throughout these books, it is the
institution of kingship which effectively controls the entire
structure of the historiography of the books of 1&2 Samuel and
1&2 Kings. Yet this illustrates still more forcibly the purely
national orientation of the ideas of divine rule which appear.
The dynastic promise made to David through the prophet Nathan
in 2 Sam 7:1-17 is the pivotal point of the entire story. At a
number of vital points in the unfolding course of events we are
told that God acts "for the sake of (his) servant David" (1 Kgs
11:12-13, 32, 34, 36; 15:4). Perhaps most striking of all is the
assertion of 2 Kgs 19:34 concerning God's intention of
protecting Jerusalem and its king in the face of the threatened
siege by Sennacherib and his forces:

> For I will defend this city to save it, for my own sake
> and for the sake of my servant David.
>
> 2 Kgs 19:34

We may suggest that this is a typically national-prophetic
view of the workings of divine providence. God acts to
preserve, or if need be punish, his people on account of their
king's actions, or misdemeanors. An even more marked
instance of this is presented by the account of the plague which
is inflicted upon Israel because of David's holding of a national
census (2 Sam 24:1-25).

It was no doubt inevitable that, in a society where the
kingship was understood to be the prime cause of either blessing

or curse upon a nation, its ideas of divine action should reflect this in very large measure. Yet there emerged in the post-exilic era a more genuinely universal way of interpreting the mind and purposes of God, through the agency of wisdom. The national, and more narrowly institutional, portrayals of God's gifts and blessings were extended into a properly universal range, without losing their relevance to the structures and institutions of society. Our argument is therefore that Jewish religious ideas and practises, and a Jewish way of life in a Gentile world, became genuine possibilities, precisely because they were not called upon to forfeit their authentic Israelite origin in order to survive. Wisdom's understanding of kingship as a feature of the created order of the universe facilitated these changes. Faith could adapt to new foreign political institutions, and it could countenance the development of new political institutions of its own, because it nurtured a tradition that a divine wisdom lay behind them. The foremost expression of that divine wisdom which controlled the political order of things was to be found in the instructions which affirmed that the institution of kingship was itself a divine gift to mankind.

Titles Available from BIBAL Press:

Ivan J. Ball, Jr., *A Rhetorical Study of Zephaniah* ISBN 0-941037-02-9 [$16.95]

Duane L. Christensen, ed., *Experiencing the Exodus* ISBN 0-941037-03-7 [$7.95]

Ronald E. Clements, *Wisdom for a Changing World: Wisdom in Old Testament Theology*
ISBN 0-941037-13-4 [$7.95]

L. R. Elliott, *The Greek Verb System: Seven-Color Chart* ISBN 0-941037-11-8 [$2.95]

Norbert F. Lohfink, S.J., *Option for the Poor: The Basic Principle of Liberation Theology in the Light of the Bible* ISBN 0-941037-00-2 [$6.95]

A. Dean McKenzie, *Sacred Images and the Millennium: Christianity and Russia (A.D. 988-1988)* ISBN 0-941037-12-6 [$7.50]

Jo Milgrom, *The Binding of Isaac: The Akedah—A Primary Symbol in Jewish Thought and Art* ISBN 0-941037-05-3 [$16.95]

William R. Scott, *A Simplified Guide to BHS (Biblia Hebraica Stuttgartensia)*
ISBN 0-941037-14-2 [$5.95]

Robert J. St. Clair, *Prayers for People Like Me* ISBN 0-941037-09-6 [$6.95]

BIBAL Monograph Series

1 *Jesus Christ According to Paul:*
   The Christologies of Paul's Undisputed Epistles and the Christology of Paul
   Scott Gambrill Sinclair ISBN 0-941037-08-8 [$12.95]

2 *Enoch and Daniel: A Form Critical and Sociological Study of Historical Apocalypses*
   Stephen Breck Reid ISBN 0-941037-07-X [$12.95]

3 *Prophecy and War in Ancient Israel: Studies in the Oracles Against the Nations*
   Duane L. Christensen ISBN 0-941037-06-1 [$14.95]

Publications in Process:

The Music of the Bible Revealed, Suzanne Haïk-Vantoura
The Inerrancy of Scripture and Other Essays, Norbert F. Lohfink, S.J.
The Stories of Genesis, Hermann Gunkel (trans. John J. Scullion, S.J.)
The Whole-Brain Bible: Resource Guide for Creative Teaching, Carole R. Fontaine, ed.

Shipping Schedule:	Up to $10	$2	
	$10-20	3	
Sales Tax 7.25%	$20-50	4	
(California residents only)	$50-100	5	
	$100+	5%	July 1990

Mail check or money order to: BIBAL Press, P.O. Box 11123
                                Berkeley, CA 94701-2123   415/799-9252

[*Please Note*: Prices subject to change without notice]